TIBETAN SPANIEL

TAIL
Richly plumed and carried
in a curl over the back.

HINDQUARTERS
Well made and strong.

HOCK
Well let down and straight
from behind.

Title Page: UK Ch. Wildhern Ice'N' Fire owned by Linda Micklethwait.

Photographers: A.E. Keil-Wizard Photography, Karen Almkinder, Toni Marie Anders, Animal Pics, Animal World Studio, Rob Beckstead, Mary Bloom, Ellen Brandt, Callea Photo, Challenge Photos, Karen Chamberlain, Close Encounters of the Furry Kind, Nancy Cook, Ellice Hauta Photography, Isabelle Francais, Judy and Tim Gard, Tim Golden, V. Hourihane, Judy Iby, Cheryl Kelly, Kohler Photography, Susan Miccio, Lisa Molen, Jon Montgomery, Tiina Pentinmäki, Herb Rosen, John Ross, Phyllis and Rowen Tabusa, Per Unden, Kerry Williamson, Britt-Inger Wolfsberg.

Distributed in the UNITED STATES to the Pet Trade by T.F.H. Publications, Inc., One T.F.H. Plaza, Neptune City, NJ 07753; distributed in the UNITED STATES to the Bookstore and Library Trade by National Book Network, Inc. 4720 Boston Way, Lanham MD 20706; in CANADA to the Pet Trade by H & L Pet Supplies Inc., 27 Kingston Crescent, Kitchener, Ontario N2B 2T6; Rolf C. Hagen Inc., 3225 Sartelon St. Laurent-Montreal Quebec H4R 1E8; in CANADA to the Book Trade by Vanwell Publishing Ltd., 1 Northrup Crescent, St. Catharines, Ontario L2M 6P5 ; in ENGLAND by T.F.H. Publications, PO Box 15, Waterlooville PO7 6BQ; in AUSTRALIA AND THE SOUTH PACIFIC by T.F.H. (Australia), Pty. Ltd., Box 149, Brookvale 2100 N.S.W., Australia; in NEW ZEALAND by Brooklands Aquarium Ltd. 5 McGiven Drive, New Plymouth, RD1 New Zealand; in Japan by T.F.H. Publications, Japan—Jiro Tsuda, 10-12-3 Ohjidai, Sakura, Chiba 285, Japan; in SOUTH AFRICA by Lopis (Pty) Ltd., P.O. Box 39127, Booysens, 2016, Johannesburg, South Africa. Published by T.F.H. Publications, Inc.

MANUFACTURED IN THE
UNITED STATES OF AMERICA
BY T.F.H. PUBLICATIONS, INC.

TIBETAN
SPANIEL

A COMPLETE AND RELIABLE HANDBOOK

Susan Miccio

RX-110

CONTENTS

INTRODUCTION TO THE TIBETAN SPANIEL

I live with eight Tibetan Spaniels, called "Tibbies" for short. If I could manage to give each the same love and affection I give an "only dog," I'd have a thousand. In fact, there's a saying among Tibbie owners: "Tibbies are like potato chips—you can't have just one!" It's a fact that many people who own one Tibbie find themselves craving another, and anyone who has shared life with a Tibbie declares that he or she will never be without a Tibbie again.

What is so special about Tibetan Spaniels? With their appealing monkey faces, uncanny intelligence and endearing mannerisms, Tibbies enchant all who

The Tibetan Spaniel's unique appearance and willful spirit make him a special addition to any household. Ch. Hysam's Runaway Train owned by John and Susan Mullins.

come to know them. People are delighted by the Tibbie's ideal size—neither too large nor too small—and are charmed by his comical antics. Even people who thought they could like only a "big dog" are disarmed by the spirit of the big dog that lives inside the Tibbie. He adapts perfectly to life either in a city apartment or a country house. He can be a rough and tumble sidekick or a gentle cuddly lap dog.

Is a Tibbie the dog for everyone? No. If you need a consistently and willingly obedient dog, one that never questions your authority and always complies with your demands, chances are the Tibetan Spaniel is not for you. However, if you could love a willful imp that usually consents to your requests but occasionally teases you, all the while grinning at you and tweaking your heart, you and the Tibetan Spaniel may be a perfect match.

The charm, intelligence and wit of the Tibetan Spaniel endear the breed to all who meet him. Aust. Ch. Toreana Galaxy Belle with owner Pam Dunlop.

DOG CHALLENGE CERTIFICATE 30

RESERVE DOG CHALLENGE CERTIFICATE 45

BITCH CHALLENGE CERTIFICATE 47

RESERVE BITCH CHALLENGE CERTIFICATE 130

BEST IN SHOW 30

BEST OPPOSITE SEX 47

SPECIAL BEST PUPPY 120

on
rawford
A.G Dic

****

President : Mr A.W Young
Treasurer : Mrs V Armstrong
Vice-Chairman : Mr K McKie

Chairman : Mrs A Young
Secretary : Mrs C Rankin
Hon.Vice Pres. : Mrs Sanderson

The Tibetan Spaniel Club of Scotland

CATALOGUE OF FIFTH CHAMPIONSHIP SHOW

32 CLASS (UNBENCHED) SINGLE BREED

(Held under Kennel Club Rules & Show Regulations)

TO BE HELD IN

THE COCHRANE HALL, ALVA

SUNDAY 26TH APRIL 1992

SHOW OPENS : 9.30 AM   JUDGING COMMENCES : 10.00 AM

JUDGE : MRS HAZEL BUTLER (COLPHILL)

Guarantors to the Kennel Club:

Mrs A Young, Nether Common, Rait, Perthshire (Chairman)
Mrs V Armstrong, Friarland Farm, by Ayr   (Treasurer)
Mrs C Rankin, 23 Fairspark Terr., Kinneil, Bo'ness, West Lothian (Secretary)
Mrs P Scott, 83 Patrick Allan Fraser St., Arbroath
Mr B Stevenson, 41 Inchmickery Rd., Dalgety Bay, Fife
Mr K McKie, 10 Hillview Rd., Darvel, Ayrshire

HON. VETERINARY SURGEON: Cameron & Greig, Ardmohr, Stirling Rd., Milnathort.
                           Tel. Kinross (0577) 63494

ROSETTES: 1st - 5th in all classes   ⊘821 670215
                BEST VETERAN

SPECIALS: SHOW SPONSORED BY PHILLIPS YEAST PRODUCTS

                Prizes to the Value of:

                £30.00 for BEST IN SHOW
                £20.00 for BEST OPPOSITE SEX
                £20.00 for BEST PUPPY

                THE TIBETAN SPANIEL CLUB OF SCOTLAND donate:

                £10.00 for BEST OPPOSITE SEX PUPPY

SHOW MANAGER: MR K McKIE

HON. SECRETARY: MRS CONNIE RANKIN, NIKNAR, 23 FAIRSPARK TERR., KINNEIL, BO'NESS, WEST LOTHIAN. TEL. 0506 823 988

HISTORY OF THE TIBETAN SPANIEL

According to myth, the Tibetan Spaniel was the "prayer dog" of Tibetan monasteries, where he was responsible for spinning the prayer wheel. Ch. Alanli's Willy The Conqueror owned by Susan Miccio.

Jigme sped down the steep, narrow steps, his hand trailing along the stone wall to his right, and plunged into a darkened passageway. The pungent odor of the yak butter lamps and the drone of chanting emitted from the narrow doorway to a chapel on the left. Hurrying on, he turned a corner and stopped abruptly, shielding his eyes with his palm and blinking at the sunlight ahead. Emerging into the open courtyard, he lowered his hand and slowed to a sedate pace. Pausing respectfully by a group of elder monks seated in a circle on the cold pavement, the young monk waited, contemplating the snap of the prayer flags flying in the brisk wind far above. Finishing his lecture, the most revered of the monks, called Rimpoche or "precious," raised his eyes to receive Jigme's message about newly arrived visitors and nodded. As he rose to his feet, his deep red and bright saffron robes swept aside to reveal two glittering brown eyes peaking from beneath their folds. The little dog also rose and shook out her silky, golden coat. She shot Jigme a glance of rebuke. He smiled and replied, "Ah,

Dolma, have I disturbed your meditation? So sorry."Placing her paw delicately on the Rimpoche's forgotten prayer wheel, lying where he had left it, she trilled softly. Retrieving the prayer wheel, Jigme whispered, "Thank you, Dolma." She grinned back at him and, with a flip of her tail, turned to follow her master, as the lion followed in Lord Buddha's footsteps.

author — Susan Miccio

IN THE HIMALAYAS

For a millennium or more, the vivacious Tibetan Spaniel has been bred to be a companion, bed warmer and watchdog in Tibet and her neighboring countries in the Himalayas. Based on the sparse photographic record, it is believed that Tibbies from different areas varied slightly in appearance, as may be expected due to the great distances between and relative isolation of many communities. Although written records are few, we also believe that they lived mainly in Buddhist monasteries and wealthy homes.

As Buddhists, Tibetans believe in reincarnation— when the body dies, the soul migrates to another body. Every living being has such a soul, Tibetans believe, and the soul in a person's body may have resided in a dog in a previous life or may yet reside in one in a future life. In Tibetan eyes, a small, lion-like dog dutifully trailing his master suggests the fierce lion faithfully following Buddha. This image symbolizes a key tenet of Buddhism—the triumph of peace over violence. This belief system is partly accountable for the Tibetans' respect and fondness for dogs, unique among Asian cultures.

Lauli-La and Chotu are "Damcis," the Tibetan Spaniel of Bhutan, a Himalayan kingdom bordering Tibet. Owner, Martina Krüger.

His Holiness the Dalai Lama, the secular and religious leader of Tibet, meets Int./Nordic Ch. Nee of Zlazano of Finland.

Since at least the seventh century (but more likely since prehistory), the people of the regions that eventually became the nations of China and Tibet have traded with one another. Dogs were among the goods they exchanged. Although we can never know for sure, we believe that the ancestors of Tibetan Spaniels were sent to China hundreds of years ago and used to develop the breed now called the Pekingese. It is also possible that small dogs favored by the Chinese were sent to Tibet where they in turn may have contributed to the Tibetan Spaniel.

Until the 20th century, Tibet was tightly closed to Westerners. Lhasa, its capital, was called the "Forbidden City." During this time, only a few explorers, missionaries, traders and adventurers from the west penetrated the mysterious country. Although their accounts mention large dogs, such as the Tibetan Mastiff, and roaming packs of "pariah" dogs, no one reported smaller companion dogs. Perhaps these visitors did not enter private homes or perhaps they did not consider the small dogs they saw noteworthy.

FROM TIBET TO GREAT BRITAIN

An unknown number of Tibetan Spaniels found their way to Great Britain in the late 19th century via

The Tibetan Spaniels seen in Great Britain in the early 1900s were often solid black or black with white markings, colors that are rare today. This Tibbie appeared in the Kennel Encyclopedia of 1911.

British citizens stationed near the Himalayas in what was then their colony of India. The earliest, most outspoken proponent of the breed was Mrs. McLaren Morrison, who brought home her first Tibetan Spaniels in 1895 and exhibited them in 1898.

In 1904, a British military expedition from India forced its way to Lhasa. A Tibbie called Lhassa, adopted by expedition member Col. F.M. Bailey, returned to India with him, walking hundreds of miles over the mountains. Lhassa later traveled to Great Britain.

As a result of the Younghusband Expedition, the British maintained a presence in Tibet until India gained independence in 1947. Although the Tibetans were reluctant to part with their companion dogs, the British managed to obtain a few Tibetan Spaniels during this period. However, those that reached Great Britain, along with their progeny, nearly died out during the World Wars.

In 1946, Sir Edward and Lady Wakefield left India with two unrelated sable Tibbies, a male called Lama and a dainty, reddish female called Dolma. The same year, Col. and Mrs. A.W. Hawkins returned home with two of Lama's littermates: Garpon, a red male, and Potala, a black-and-tan female. All Tibbies in the west are descended from these four dogs born in Asia and a single British-born dog called Skyid, a red male left from the pre-War lines.

In 1951, the Chinese invaded and occupied Tibet. The Dalai Lama, who is the secular and religious leader of Tibet, escaped to India in 1959, together with 100,000 of his followers. Since then, we believe that most Tibetan Spaniels (and other small native breeds) in Tibet have died or were deliberately killed by the Chinese. The few western travelers permitted to enter Tibet since the takeover have reported only a tiny number of what appear to be purebred dogs. Outside Tibet, some have survived in communities of Tibetan refugees.

Between the World Wars, Dr. A.R.H. Grieg sent Tibbies from India, where she worked near the Tibetan frontier, home to Great Britain. Only one of these Tibbie descendants survived to contribute to today's bloodlines.

While the Tibetan Spaniel was disappearing from his homeland, British fanciers nurtured and preserved the breed. Careful breeding of close relatives brought the number of Tibbies up to 58 by 1958. In the late 1960s and early '70s, breeders managed to add a handful of Tibetan Spaniels, brought from India, Nepal and Hong Kong, to western bloodlines.

Today, nearly 400 Tibetan Spaniels are registered with the British Kennel Club each year. At Crufts 1997 (the UK's most prestigious show), 177 Tibetan Spaniels competed. Although about 100 kennels are now active in the UK, most produce only one or two litters each year. Kennels that have figured prominently in pedigrees of recent years include Mrs. Ann Wynyard's

13

Braeduke, the Amcross Kennel of Miss M.C. Hourihane and Mrs. Deirdre Jenkins and Mrs. Linda Micklethwait's Wildhern. However, note that many other fine British kennels have made their mark in Tibetan Spaniels, both at home and abroad.

TO OTHER COUNTRIES

After concentrating on building the breed for a few years, the British began to export to other countries. The first exports went to Sweden in 1956. Her neighbors, Finland and Norway, began importing in 1964 and 1974 respectively. Tibbies soon became very popular in the Nordic countries. For example, over 1000 puppies are registered in Finland each year, and the Tibetan Spaniel usually ranks in the top ten most popular breeds. Hundreds of kennels are active in these countries, although most produce fairly few puppies per year.

By the 1980s, the Tibetan Spaniel had spread to most European countries, including Denmark, France, the Netherlands and Ireland. Today, a small cadre of breeders in these countries cultivate moderately growing populations. On the continent, breeders and exhibitors often travel between countries to show their Tibbies.

Tibetan Spaniels have become very popular in the Nordic countries. Int./Nordic Ch. Sagaland's Z-Mar-Tell owned by Gerd and Kjell Strand has been the top-winning Tibbie in Norway from 1993–1996.

Tibbies have existed in Australia and New Zealand since the early 1970s. Aust. Ch. Toreana Szo-Fei owned by Joan Aspinall is not only a top-winning bitch but also a therapy dog.

In the southern hemisphere, Tibbies have lived in Australia and New Zealand since the early 1970s. Breeders there tend to rely on homebred stock but occasionally import from one another or from other countries. The recent formation of a Tibetan Spaniel club in Australia, the only one in the southern hemisphere, bodes well for the future of the breed there.

Breeders in Canada have been encouraged to preserve the breed in that country. The top Tibetan Spaniel in Canada, Can. Ch. Rivervalley's Tao Zen Spirit is owned by Linda Matthews.

Canada and South Africa are examples of countries where the breed has been around for several years but has never really "caught on." The few breeders struggle to preserve the breed. Although many countries around the world report no registrations of Tibetan Spaniels, the breed continues to

ALGONQUIN

BEST OF BREED BEST PUPPY IN BREED

SEPTEMBER 1996

JOHN ROSS PHOTO

TIBETAN SPANIEL
CLUB OF AMERICA
FEBRUARY 1997

BEST
OF
BREED
KOHLER

ted owners from all over the world share news and answer each others' questions online through the Tibetan Spaniel Global Village. Details on joining the Village are available at the home page above.

Another worthy organization is the International Tibetan Spaniel Working Party (ITSWP). The ITSWP is made up of contact representatives from almost all nations where Tibbies live. Its mission is to monitor the breed worldwide and to collate information that will help breeders to produce only healthy, sound puppies that will become lovable companions.

Although US Tibetan Spaniel breeders are small in number, they have been dedicated to the development of the breed. Ch. Ambrier Boda Zelicious Zima owned by Mallory Cosby Driskill and Betty Wrenn Hoggard.

DESCRIPTION OF THE TIBETAN SPANIEL

Where even the valleys are 14,000 feet or more above sea level and the peaks soar to nearly 30,000 feet, the climate on the plateau of Tibet is one of the most challenging on Earth. The air is oxygen-poor, but the wind is persistent. Temperatures reach only 50º Fahrenheit in summer and plunge to -40º Fahrenheit in winter. This is where the Tibetan Spaniel evolved. The sturdy, smart and adaptable Tibetan Spaniel survived and thrived where no weak or dull-witted dog could.

BACK TO NATURE

It is easy to look at the Tibetan Spaniel and see only a petite form and pixie face, easy to think of him as

The hardy and adaptable Tibetan Spaniel evolved and thrived for centuries in the rugged mountainous climate of Tibet. Fin. Ch. Chu-Shun Lejja owned by Tiina Pentinmäki.

"only" a lap dog. While the Tibbie has many of the endearing qualities of the toy dogs, the truth is that he is closer to his "roots" in the wild. His body is built for both speed and stamina. His senses are attuned to survival, and he relies on his sharp eyes and keen ears as much as his nose. His versatile brain is adept at problem-solving. Though he loves his human companions, he is also willing to strike out on his own.

The Tibetan Spaniel has a low reproductive rate. Females go into "season" less often than most breeds. Their litters tend to be small—about four or five puppies—and the puppies tend to mature at a slower

pace than most breeds. For example, a Tibbie puppy is rarely ready to go to a new home until he is ten weeks old.

A Tibbie's body, viewed from the side, is rectangular. Ch. Wildhern Full Of Fire owned by Herb Rosen.

APPEALING APPEARANCE

A Tibbie looks like a puppy all his life. His highly expressive face is capable of smiling, frowning and pouting. The shining, dark brown eyes are positioned to look straight forward. The muzzle is short (but not flat), blunt and filled out with cushioning in the lips. The teeth are slightly undershot—that is, the upper incisors fit inside the lower incisors. Unlike the other Tibetan breeds (the Lhasa Apso, Tibetan Terrier and Shih Tzu), the facial hair is short and smooth. The small drop ears are set moderately high and lift to attractively frame the face.

The Tibbie comes in all colors. Ch. Dragonhold Gandharva's sable coat is the most common, while Ch. Jo'Jevon Pirate of Dragonhold's black coat is a rarity. Owners, Cheryl Kelly and J. Wright, J. Child, and Y. Crofts.

A Tibbie's body, viewed from the side, is rectangular. He stands about ten inches at the shoulder and is slightly longer than he is high. The head is small in proportion to the body. The tail arches over the back and falls to one side or the other. Viewed from the front, the forelegs are slightly bowed. His ideal weight is between nine and fifteen pounds. The well-built Tibbie neither waddles nor wiggles but strides efficiently and briskly about his business.

The paws are distinctive. Called "hare-feet," the two middle toes are longer than the outside toes, causing the paw to appear elongated and flat. The hare-foot design gives the Tibbie speed. Since his weight rests on the central pad, his toes are free for gripping. This makes him sure-footed and dexterous. In fact, a Tibbie often uses his forepaws like hands. In the adult, hair growing from the top of the toes extends beyond their tips until it eventually takes on the appearance of a pointed "slipper." Hair also grows profusely between the pads, creating a "snowshoe" or "glove" to protect the pads.

COAT OF MANY COLORS

The Tibbie has a "double coat." The short, fluffy undercoat lies close to the skin for insulation. The overcoat is made up of guard hairs. Lying fairly flat over the undercoat, the long guard hairs are soft but protect the dog from the elements. Fully mature males develop a "mane" of longer, fuller hair surrounding the neck and shoulders, while a less extensive "shawl" covers the adult female's shoulders. "Trousers" ("skirts" for the ladies) or "pantaloons," which are fringes of longer hair, grow from the buttocks. In addition to the gloves described earlier, silky fringes also grow from the back of the forelegs and from the ears. The hair on the tail grows into a long plume.

A young puppy usually has a fairly short, plush coat with only the suggestion of the mane/shawl and fringes that will grow in later. Over the next two to three years, he progresses through stages of more or less coat. The adult coat may not develop fully until the Tibbie is between two and four years old. Throughout their lives, both males and females may shed their undercoats once or twice a year and unspayed females lose coat after their seasons and while raising puppies.

The Tibbie's coat comes in all colors. The most common, called a "sable," is made up of various shades of yellow, ranging from a pale biscuit to a bright reddish-gold, and accented with black hairs. This black sabling may be either pronounced, with heavy infusions of black throughout the mane/shawl and ear fringes, or minimal, with black barely noticeable at the tips of the ear fringes. The trousers and other fringes may be a lighter shade than the rest of the coat.

The next most common color is the "particolor." He is predominantly white with patches of brown, gold, black or red on his head and body. The "black-and-tan" is predominantly black with tan points, most noticeably above the eyes. The black-and-tan with

Thor has the "Buddha mark" on his forehead. The mark often diminishes or disappears as puppies mature. Owner, Toni Marie Anders.

white markings is called a "tricolor." Black (with or without white markings but no tan), ruby red and silver (gray) coats are also beautiful but rare. Sables and a few particolors have dominated the color scheme for many years, but some breeders are currently striving to restore the rarer colors.

With the exception of the particolor, it is difficult to determine the adult color based on the color of the puppy. For example, newborn puppies that are chestnut-colored or near-black may lighten to a pale gold sable by the time they are three months old. Typically, a puppy's white markings, such as his socks or a thumbprint-shaped "Buddha mark" on the forehead,

Ch. Tibroke's Stallone of Avalon owned by Becky Sumner is a beautiful example of a tri-colored Tibetan Spaniel.

may diminish or even disappear. Similarly, a puppy born with a black mask covering the whole face may retain only a hint of black on the tip of his muzzle when he turns one year old.

The "scowl," another distinctive feature, is an X-shaped marking, sketched out by darker hairs, between the Tibbie's eyes. Most visible on sables, the upper arms of the X sometimes arch up and over the eyes like eyebrows. The name of the marking is a bit misleading. Rather than give him a grumpy look, the scowl actually enhances the Tibbie's already comical, monkey-like expression by adding just a hint of impishness.

The Tibetan Spaniel's distinctive X-shaped "scowl" is evident on Shavarin's Doremi's forehead. Owner, Tiina Pentinmäki.

STANDARD FOR THE TIBETAN SPANIEL

The American breed standard and most of the world's other standards for our breed are based substantially on the breed standard written by the Tibetan Spaniel Association (UK) and approved by the Kennel Club of Great Britain. The most recent version came out in 1986. In addition to their official breed standards, the Tibetan Spaniel Club of America and other breed clubs around the world have published illustrated breed standards. These documents supplement and explain the breed standard's narrative with the help of drawings. All other published interpretations of the breed standards are the personal opinions of their authors and, as such, are unofficial and non-binding.

General Appearance—Should be small, active and alert. The outline should give a well balanced appearance, slightly longer in body than the height at withers. *Fault*—Coarseness of type.

Size, Proportion, Substance—*Size*—Height about 10 inches. Body slightly longer from the point of shoulder to root of tail than the height at withers. Weight 9—15 pounds being ideal.

Head—Small in proportion to body and proudly carried, giving an impression of quality. Masculine in dogs but free from coarseness. *Eyes*—dark brown in color, oval in shape, bright and expressive, of medium size set fairly well apart but forward looking, giving an apelike *expression*. Eye rims black. *Faults*—Large full eyes; light eyes; mean expression. *Ears* medium size, pendant, well feathered in the adult and set fairly high. They may have a slight lift from the skull, but should not fly. Large, heavy, low set ears are not typical.

Skull slightly domed, moderate width and length. *Faults*—Very domed or flat wide skull. *Stop* slight, but defined. Medium length of *muzzle*, blunt with cushioning, free from wrinkle. The *chin* should show some depth and width. *Faults*—Accentuated stop; long, plain down face, without stop; broad flat muzzle; pointed, weak or wrinkled muzzle. Black nose preferred. *Faults*—Liver or putty-colored pigmentation.

Mouth ideally slightly undershot, the upper incisors fitting neatly inside and touching the lower incisors.

In 1996, Fin./Dan./Sw. Ch. Simpasture Biko-Suku-Na was named Tibetan Spaniel of the Year in Finland. Owners, Tiia Stenberg and Päivi Säviaho.

Teeth should be evenly placed and the lower jaw wide between the canine tusks. Full dentition desired. A level mouth is permissible, providing there is sufficient width and depth of chin to preserve the blunt appearance of the muzzle. Teeth must not show when mouth is closed. *Faults*—Overshot mouth; protruding tongue.

Neck, Topline, Body—*Neck* moderately short, strong and well set on. Level back. Well ribbed with good depth. *Tail* set high, richly plumed and carried in a gay curl over the back when moving. Should not be penalized for dropping tail when standing.

Forequarters—Shoulder well placed. The bones of the forelegs slightly bowed but firm at shoulder. Moderate bone. *Faults*—Very bowed or loose front. Dewclaws may be removed. *Feet* hare-footed, small and neat. *Fault*—Cat feet.

Hindquarters—Well made and strong. Stifle well developed, showing moderate angulation. Hocks well let down and straight when viewed from behind. *Faults*—Straight stifle; cow hocks. Dewclaws may be removed. *Feet* as in front.

Coat—Double coat, silky in texture, smooth on face and front of legs, of moderate length on body, but lying rather flat. Ears and back of forelegs nicely

The overall appearance of the Tibetan Spaniel is one of a small, active, well-balanced dog with an alert and intelligent expression. UK Ch. Wildhern's Ice' N' Fire owned by Linda Micklethwait.

Åskmolets Goliat, a parti-colored Tibetan Spaniel owned by Britt-Inger Wolfsberg, was the second top-winning Tibbie in Sweden in 1996.

feathered, tail and buttocks well furnished with longer hair. Neck covered with a mane or "shawl" of longer hair which is more pronounced in dogs than bitches. Feathering between toes often extending beyond the feet. Should not be over-coated and bitches tend to carry less coat and mane than dogs. *Presentation—* In the show ring it is essential the Tibetan Spaniel be presented in an unaltered condition with the coat lying naturally with no teasing, parting or stylizing of the hair. Specimens where the coat has been altered by trimming, clipping, or by artificial means shall be so severely penalized as to be effectively eliminated from competition. Dogs with such a long coat that there is no rectangle of daylight showing beneath, or so profuse that it obstructs the natural outline, are to be severely penalized. Whiskers are not to be removed. Hair growing between the pads on the underside of the feet may be trimmed for safety and cleanliness.

Color—All colors, and mixtures of colors allowed. *Feet*—White markings allowed.

Gait—Quick moving, straight, free, positive.

Temperament—Gay and assertive, highly intelligent, aloof with strangers. *Fault*—Nervousness.

Approved May 10, 1983
Reformatted February 7, 1989

LIVING WITH A TIBETAN SPANIEL

While most people are initially attracted to the Tibetan Spaniel because of his compact size and charming appearance, they soon become fascinated by his enigmatic personality. One Tibbie owner summed it up when he suggested that if a group of lions is called a pride, we should call a group of Tibbies an "attitude." How true!

When the British first saw Tibbies in India, they probably called them "spaniels" only because the dogs were about the same size and served the same purpose as the toy spaniels back home. Despite the "spaniel" in his name, Tibbies are not driven by instinct to hunt like spaniel breeds such as the Brittany or Springer. First and foremost, Tibbies are companion dogs and secondly, watchdogs.

A COMEDIAN WITH AN INTELLECT

A highly intelligent dog that needs lots of mental stimulation and physical action, the Tibetan Spaniel is easily bored by monotonous drills but loves challenging games. As a big tease, he constantly plots to

Perhaps due to their playful spirit, Tibbies are fascinated with toys. As Travis demonstrates, most Tibbies won't go anywhere without their teddy bears! Owner, Stephanie Alleman.

The Tibetan Spaniel often uses his considerable intellect and problem solving skills to tease his friends. You can usually tell by his expression that your Tibbie is up to something! Ch. Krisala's Petite Gourmet owned by Becky Maag.

outwit you and the other family pets. One of my Tibbies delights in annoying the others by dangling a treat before them. Then, when they grab for it, she snatches the treat away at the last moment and taunts them with laughing eyes. Another deliberately provokes her brothers into a dispute over a toy. While they argue and wrestle, she kidnaps the toy and escapes to a hideaway. Most Tibbies put their considerable intellect to good use in such exploits.

The Tibetan Spaniel forgets nothing. He recognizes friends, human or canine, years after last seeing them. Past slights and insults may be forgiven but they are certainly not forgotten.

Perhaps because of their need for interesting play, Tibbies adore toys. Chew toys such as Nylabone® products are fun and safe. The Tibbie is especially fond of fuzzies with squeakers. Few Tibbies are ever without their teddy bears or other plush toys. They carry them everywhere, present them to visitors, take them to bed, and use them as pillows. A Tibbie cannot possibly have too many toys.

The Tibbie is a great communicator. He has a decent bark (not a yap), ranging from a deep "woof" (that sounds like a much larger dog) to a higher pitched "arf," that he uses depending on whether he is warning off an intruder or saying "hello" to a friend.

The talkative Tibbie also has an amazing variety of other vocalizations with which he expresses himself. He grunts, grumbles, trills, whines, snorts and yips. He even makes a rolling "r" sound. One of my girls has a special bark that means, "I want it, NOW" followed by a snort as an exclamation point. There can be no mistaking her meaning!

A Tibbie loves the comforts of home and can often be found in his favorite position — sleeping on his back. Owner, Kolly Pascale-Badan.

A FELINE CANINE

Many of the Tibetan Spaniel's habits are distinctly cat-like. He is a curious, clever (some say conniving) creature. He likes to open doors and investigate what's on the other side. He has no fear of heights and will find the highest spot to recline and contemplate. Tibbies have even been known to climb trees and scale fences. Although he gets dirty and disheveled while playing outdoors, he prefers to be clean and neat. In fact, if my Tibbie's trousers are soiled and he can't tidy himself up, he may sit down and refuse to budge until I, his willing servant, attend to the matter. It is not unusual to see a Tibbie grooming himself and washing his face with his forepaw, like a cat.

The Tibbie loves his comforts. He is the consummate bed dog. I awake each winter morning with my Tibbies curled up next to me, one delightfully warm body on each side. Another sleeps on her back on her own pillow next to mine. This arrangement is not at all unusual among Tibbie owners!

Whenever they weren't keeping someone warm in old Tibet, we believe that Tibbies kept vigil on the flat rooftops of the houses or patrolled the high monastery walls. When they spotted approaching strangers, they barked to alert the Tibetan Mastiffs below. Even in a modern household, the family Tibbie typically takes up position on the back of the sofa or on a table

Known for his sense of humor, the Tibetan Spaniel can usually be found performing for his adoring fans.

in front of a window to keep an eye on his territory. He is a superb watch dog with keen eyesight and hearing. Over the years, I have learned to trust my Tibbies' watchful instincts. Even if I cannot see or hear what they are worried about, I know that they rarely raise a false alarm.

With smiles and wagging tails, most Tibbies greet anyone who comes through the door. Other Tibbies are slightly more suspicious. When a stranger first approaches him, a Tibbie may be aloof, averting his eyes or turning his head away. However, when he sees that his owner accepts the stranger, he will generally become friendly within a few minutes.

A HARD HEAD WITH A SOFT HEART

Although individuals vary, the Tibetan Spaniel is basically an independent breed. In contrast to breeds known for their obedience, such as the Border Collie or Golden Retriever, independent breeds are less interested in pleasing you than in getting their own way. The Tibbie considers anything you give him as simply his due and not something for that he should be unduly grateful. A willingness to strike out on his own and the intelligence to figure out how to go about it are

Although they can be stubborn, Tibbies are also very compassionate and sensitive, making them wonderful therapy dogs. Danny (Ch. Bet' R's Standing Ovation, CD) helps his friend Lori Kloss complete a race during the Special Olympics. Owner, Rod Beckstead.

traits that enabled the Tibetan Spaniel to survive in old Tibet. For today's pet owner, a Tibbie's headstrong behavior makes him a fascinating but occasionally frustrating companion.

The greatest drawback of the Tibbie's independent streak is his tendency to run away—perhaps in pursuit of some prize but sometimes, I suspect, just to assert his autonomy. Because accidents are a leading cause of death in our breed, you must take sensible precautions to prevent your Tibbie's escape. Spay or neuter your pet so that attractive members of the opposite sex are not a temptation. Teach him basic obedience using positive techniques, keep gates and exterior doors tightly closed and fence your yard. Because most Tibbies are capable of climbing and tunneling, make sure that your fencing will stymie any escape artist. Finally, never, ever allow your Tibbie off his lead in an unfenced area without *proven* offlead training and *constant* supervision.

Your Tibbie's occasional hard-headedness is easy to excuse because of his many other redeeming qualities. He is sensitive. He knows when you are suffering, physically or emotionally. At these times, he wants nothing more than to be by your side. This selfless compassion makes the Tibetan Spaniel an ideal therapy dog. He is the perfect size to cuddle in someone's lap or lay alongside in a bed. A Tibbie called Pippin works with severely disabled persons who are unable to speak by responding to commands they key into electronic speaking devices. "Cakes" comforts patients suffering from Alzheimer disease, while "Kylee" consoles children undergoing painful cancer treatments. "Holly" helps the human therapists with their patient's rehabilitation exercises. These are just a few examples. All over the world, owners and their therapy Tibbies bring pleasure to lonely or suffering people.

One of the most frustrating and dangerous drawbacks of Tibbie ownership is the dog's tendency to run away. Make sure your Tibbie is always in a secure area when off lead.

Kiri, an exuberant puppy with no "off" switch, sits motionless in the laps of nursing home residents as they pet her. She barely flinches when a woman, who suffers from involuntary muscle spasms, accidentally strikes her in the face. Kiri's behavior is typical. Therapy Tibbies always understand when they are "on the job." They are patient, gentle and sweet. They know just what to do.

Patients are equally devoted to their Tibbies. When "Dreamer" contracted a skin disorder, her owner regretfully announced that she planned to stop Dreamer's visits to a nursing home. Residents and staff of the home joined to vehemently protest her decision. "If Dreamer can overlook our problems, we can overlook hers," they argued. Dreamer's owner relented. Dreamer still pays her visits and loves every minute with her patients.

Children are attracted to Tibbies because of their small size and appealing appearance. If socialized to youngsters while puppies, Tibbies make affectionate playmates for children. However, because Tibbies are small, rough handling by a child may severely injure or frighten them. Therefore, breeders carefully screen potential buyers who have small children, especially toddlers, to assure that the children know how to be gentle and kind to dogs.

If properly socialized as puppies, Tibetan Spaniels make wonderful companions for children due to their small size and high energy level. Sarah Sheppard with her best friend Gizmo (UK Ch. Tibanchi Dashing Debonair).

Tibbies of my own breeding live peaceably with a variety of other family pets including cats, parrots, ferrets and large and small dogs of many breeds. However, you should take sensible precautions in multi-species households—both to protect smaller creatures from the Tibbie and to protect the Tibbie from larger animals.

The Tibetan Spaniel has absolutely no concept of his own smallness. He will play with, tease or challenge a big dog as readily as another Tibbie or small dog. Although large dogs and Tibbies in the same family almost always get along just fine, it's a good idea to supervise Tibbies and larger dogs. Sadly, some families have learned this lesson the hard way when their Tibbies were injured.

As long as they are closely supervised, allow your Tibbie to make friends with all different kinds of people and animals. Fin. Ch. Shavarin's Arsene greets a lamb. Owner, Tiina Pentinmäki.

Tibetan Spaniels greet other Tibbies and members of other Tibetan breeds with greater enthusiasm than other kinds of dogs. It is obvious that they recognize their own kind. There is special pleasure in a multi-Tibbie household. Tibbies play together vigorously and carry on conversations in "Tibbie speak." One of them will normally establish himself (or herself) as dominant, and this "top dog" demands respect and obedience from everyone. It has been my experience that living in a Tibbie "attitude" (pack) is emotionally healthy for the dogs but does not in any way detract from the loving relationship between the Tibbies and their owner.

GOING OUT AND ABOUT

Tibbies love the outdoors. If they have a chance to be off-lead in a safe place, Tibbies will run flat out, their tails curling and uncurling and their backs arching with each stride—a truly beautiful sight. They also enjoy a casual stroll with lots of stops for sniffing.

Give your Tibbie routine exercise. A healthy, fit Tibbie is capable of jogging or walking briskly by your side for miles. Even if you have a fenced area, it's a good idea to take your Tibbie for a walk at least once a day. It will keep both of you in shape. However, if you are unable to exercise him outdoors, play energetic games like "Fetch" indoors.

Generally, Tibbies are all-weather dogs. Most thrive in cold weather, down to about 10º Fahrenheit, and they adore snow. Some of my best memories are of taking my Tibbies out after a snowfall and watching them leap through deep snow like gazelles, the flakes dusting them like powdered sugar. Although some

Opposite: An all-weather dog, the Tibetan Spaniel enjoys both the snow and the sun. Lady Jo, owned by Ellen Brandt, works on her tan.

Tibbies love to be outdoors and need daily exercise to keep healthy and fit. Arthur (UK Ch. What Next at Nimana) enjoys a run in the park. Owner, Kerry Williamson.

Tibbies like to bask in the sun, most become lethargic when the temperature climbs to 90º and above. Ironically, many Tibbies detest getting their paws wet and refuse to step out in the rain or walk on dewy grass.

Tibbies are generally good travelers and readily accompany you on long trips or short hops. Carsickness in puppies is usually a passing phase that is well over by the time they reach three or four months old. For his safety and yours, crate your Tibbie while in the car, but in warm weather, leave him at home. The temperature in a car, even with the windows cracked, can reach lethal levels in a few minutes.

GROOMING YOUR TIBETAN SPANIEL

Books on many other breeds devote many pages to grooming— not so a Tibbie book! A Tibbie requires little grooming, and almost all owners tend to this chore themselves. It's easy. Start by accustoming your puppy to brushing and combing early in his life. Also, handle his paws frequently so that he will readily accept nail-trimming. Teach him to let you open his mouth and clean his teeth. Use food rewards and profuse praise to reinforce these lessons.

Because Tibbies live indoors under prolonged artificial light, the coat tends to shed slightly year-round. They may also "blow" their undercoat once or twice a year. To minimize shedding, give your Tibbie a quick brushing every day or two. At the same time, comb through the trousers, under the belly and behind the ears to prevent mats from forming. Use a brush with natural or blunted wire bristles about one inch long.

Grooming a Tibbie is an easy task — one that most owners take care of themselves. Anu Siponen, a junior handler, practices grooming Cessy.

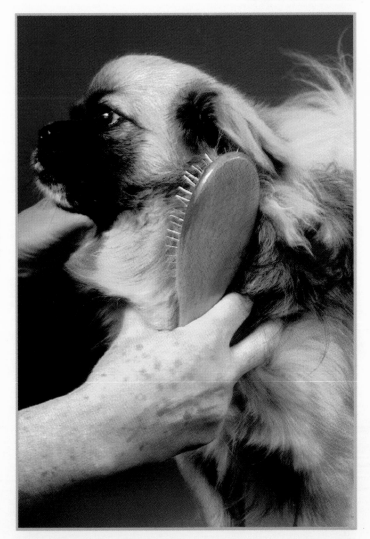

A quick daily brushing will help minimize shedding and keep your Tibbie's coat free from mats.

The healthy Tibbie has no "doggy" odor. Still, bathe your Tibbie regularly once every three or four weeks. Before his bath, brush him and gently remove any mats you find. Because of the double coat, make sure you wet him all the way down to the skin. Apply a mild shampoo made for dogs and squeeze it through the coat. Don't scrub or rough up the coat while shampooing. It is extremely important to rinse thoroughly, because any shampoo left in the coat may irritate the skin. For extra silkiness and sheen, apply a conditioning rinse or spray conditioner. You may either blow dry the coat or, if the weather is warm, let your Tibbie air dry. The final step is to brush out the coat.

It is very important to trim your Tibbie's nails periodically. How often depends on how fast they grow and how much he exercises on rough surfaces. Use a plier-type trimmer for small dogs. Although some of these are equipped with a guard to prevent clipping the nail too short (that is, into the quick), do not rely on the guard. Most Tibbies have light-colored nails, so you can see the pink, triangular quick inside the nail. Trim just beyond the quick.

Bath day is a good time to examine your Tibbie's mouth and ears for any signs of trouble, such as unusual spots, bleeding gums or reddened skin. Brush his teeth once or twice a week. If needed, clean his ears using an ear cleanser made for dogs. I also recommend applying a drying agent, such as ear powder. While you're at it, run your hands over his body to check for lumps or bumps.

Do not trim your Tibbie's coat. Unless there is a diagnosed medical problem, don't remove hair from the ears either. The sole exception is to trim the hair that grows between the pads on the underside of the paw. Clipping this hair off even with the pads may help prevent fungal growth and keeps the paw free of mats and from mud, tar or other debris. *Note*: Do not trim the hair that grows from the top of the paw. This "slipper" is a breed trait that you should preserve.

When caring for your Tibetan Spaniel's feet, it is important to leave the hair on top of the paw alone. This will retain his "slipper-like" feet, a breed trait. Owner, Susan Miccio.

YOUR PUPPY'S NEW HOME

Before actually collecting your puppy, it is better that you purchase the basic items you will need in advance of the pup's arrival date. This allows you more opportunity to shop around and ensure you have exactly what you want rather than having to buy lesser quality in a hurry.

Before bringing your new Tibbie puppy home from the breeders, make sure both your family and your household are prepared for your new arrival. Owner, Tiina Pentinmäki.

It is always better to collect the puppy as early in the day as possible. In most instances this will mean that the puppy has a few hours with your family before it is time to retire for his first night's sleep away from his former home.

If the breeder is local, then you may not need any form of box to place the puppy in when you bring him home. A member of the family can hold the pup in his lap—duly protected by some towels just in case the puppy becomes car sick! Be sure to advise the breeder at what time you hope to arrive for the puppy, as this will obviously influence the feeding of the pup that morning or afternoon. If you arrive early in the day, then they will likely only give the pup a light breakfast so as to reduce the risk of travel sickness.

If the trip will be of a few hours duration, you should take a travel crate with you. The crate will provide your pup with a safe place to lie down and rest during the trip. During the trip, the puppy will no doubt wish to relieve his bowels, so you will have to make a few stops. On a long journey you may need a rest yourself,

Provide your Tibetan Spaniel puppy with plenty of toys to play with; be careful of toys with squeakies or with small parts that can break off and be swallowed.

and can take the opportunity to let the puppy get some fresh air. However, do not let the puppy walk where there may have been a lot of other dogs because he might pick up an infection. Also, if he relieves his bowels at such a time, do not just leave the feces where they were dropped. This is the height of irresponsibility. It has resulted in many public parks and other places actually banning dogs. You can purchase poop-scoops from your pet shop and should have them with you whenever you are taking the dog out where he might foul a public place.

Your journey home should be made as quickly as possible. If it is a hot day, be sure the car interior is amply supplied with fresh air. It should never be too hot or too cold for the puppy. The pup must never be placed where he might be subject to a draft. If the journey requires an overnight stop at a motel, be aware that other guests will not appreciate a puppy crying half the night. You must regard the puppy as a baby and comfort him so he does not cry for long periods. The worst thing you can do is to shout at or smack him. This will mean your relationship is off to a really bad start. You wouldn't smack a baby, and your puppy is still very much just this.

ON ARRIVING HOME

By the time you arrive home the puppy may be very tired, in which case he should be taken to his sleeping area and allowed to rest. Children should not be allowed to interfere with the pup when he is sleeping. If the pup is not tired, he can be allowed to investigate his new home—but always under your close supervision. After a short look around,

Your Tibbie may be tired from his journey when you first arrive home, so limit visitors and give him a chance to rest and relax—in his favorite position. Owners, Phyllis and Rowen Tabusa.

the puppy will no doubt appreciate a light meal and a drink of water. Do not overfeed him at his first meal because he will be in an excited state and more likely to be sick.

Although it is an obvious temptation, you should not invite friends and neighbors around to see the new arrival until he has had at least 48 hours in which to settle down. Indeed, if you can delay this longer then do so, especially if the puppy is not fully vaccinated. At the very least, the visitors might introduce some local bacteria on their clothing that the puppy is not immune to. This aspect is always a risk when a pup has been moved some distance, so the fewer people the pup meets in the first week or so the better.

DANGERS IN THE HOME

Your home holds many potential dangers for a little mischievous puppy, so you must think about these in

The great outdoors can hold many dangers for your small Tibbie pup so closely supervise her when she is outside. Flora owned by Kerry Williamson investigates the flowers.

Puppies love to chew on things, so make sure that all electrical appliances are neatly hidden from view and unplugged when not in use.

advance and be sure he is protected from them. The more obvious are as follows:

Open Fires. All open fires should be protected by a mesh screen guard so there is no danger of the pup being burned by spitting pieces of coal or wood.

Electrical Wires. Puppies just love chewing on things, so be sure that all electrical appliances are neatly hidden from view and are not left plugged in when not in use. It is not sufficient simply to turn the plug switch to the off position—pull the plug from the socket.

Open Doors. A door would seem a pretty innocuous object, yet with a strong draft it could kill or injure a puppy easily if it is slammed shut. Always ensure there is no risk of this happening. It is most likely during warm weather when you have windows or outside doors open and a sudden gust of wind blows through.

Balconies. If you live in a high-rise building, obviously the pup must be protected from falling. Be sure he cannot get through any railings on your patio, balcony, or deck.

Ponds and Pools. A garden pond or a swimming pool is a very dangerous place for a little puppy to be near. Be sure it is well screened so there is no risk of the pup falling in. It takes barely a minute for a pup— or a child—to drown.

The Kitchen. While many puppies will be kept in the kitchen, at least while they are toddlers and not able to control their bowel movements, this is a room full of danger—especially while you are cooking. When cooking, keep the puppy in a play pen or in another room where he is safely out of harm's way. Alternatively, if you have a carry box or crate, put him in this so he can still see you but is well protected.

Be aware, when using washing machines, that more than one puppy has clambered in and decided to have a nap and received a wash instead! If you leave the washing machine door open and leave the room for any reason, then be sure to check inside the machine before you close the door and switch on.

Small Children. Toddlers and small children should never be left unsupervised with puppies. In spite of such advice it is amazing just how many people not only do this but also allow children to pull and maul pups. They should be taught from the outset that a puppy is not a plaything to be dragged about the home—and they should be promptly scolded if they disobey.

Children must be shown how to lift a puppy so it is safe. Failure by you to correctly educate your children about dogs could one day result in their getting a very nasty bite or scratch. When a puppy is lifted, his weight must always be supported. To lift the pup, first place your right hand under his chest but take care not to push his elbows away from his chest wall. Next, secure the pup by using your left hand to hold his bottom. Now you can lift him and bring him close to your chest. Never lift a pup by his ears and, while he can be lifted by the scruff of his neck where the fur is loose, there is no reason ever to do this, so don't.

Beyond the dangers already cited you may be able to think of other ones that are specific to your home—steep basement steps or the like. Go around your home and check out all potential problems—you'll be glad you did.

THE FIRST NIGHT

The first few nights a puppy spends away from his mother and littermates are quite traumatic for him. He will feel very lonely, maybe cold, and will certainly miss the heartbeat of his siblings when sleeping. To help overcome his loneliness it may help to place a clock next to his bed—one with a loud tick. This will in some way soothe him, as the clock ticks to a rhythm not dissimilar from a heart beat. A cuddly toy may also

Your Tibbie puppy will miss the company of his dam and littermates in his new home. Pay special attention to him during this lonely time.

help in the first few weeks. A dim nightlight may provide some comfort to the puppy, because his eyes will not yet be fully able to see in the dark. The puppy may want to leave his bed for a drink or to relieve himself.

If the pup does whimper in the night, there are two things you should not do. One is to get up and chastise him, because he will not understand why you are shouting at him; and the other is to rush to comfort him every time he cries because he will quickly realize that if he wants you to come running all he needs to do is to holler loud enough!

By all means give your puppy some extra attention on his first night, but after this quickly refrain from so doing. The pup will cry for a while but then settle down and go to sleep. Some pups are, of course, worse than others in this respect, so you must use balanced judgment in the matter. Many owners take their pups to bed with them, and there is certainly nothing wrong with this.

The pup will be no trouble in such cases. However, you should only do this if you intend to let this be a permanent arrangement, otherwise it is hardly fair to the puppy. If you have decided to have two puppies, then they will keep each other company and you will have few problems.

OTHER PETS

If you have other pets in the home then the puppy must be introduced to them under careful supervision. Puppies will get on just fine with any other pets—but you must make due allowance for the respective sizes of the pets concerned, and appreciate that your puppy has a rather playful nature. It would be very foolish to leave him with a young rabbit. The pup will want to play and might bite the bunny and get altogether too rough with it. Kittens are more able to defend themselves from overly cheeky pups, who will get a quick scratch if they overstep the mark. The

As long as they are properly introduced, Tibetan Spaniels get along well with other pets. Indy the cockatoo is grooming Camellia's ears for her. Ouch! Owners, John and Susan Mullins.

adult cat could obviously give the pup a very bad scratch, though generally cats will jump clear of pups and watch them from a suitable vantage point. Eventually they will meet at ground level where the cat will quickly hiss and box a puppy's ears. The pup will soon learn to respect an adult cat; thereafter they will probably develop into great friends as the pup matures into an adult dog.

Don't let his innocent look fool you! A Tibbie pup is especially inquisitive and mischievous and needs you, his owner, to discipline him.

THE EARLY DAYS

You will no doubt be given much advice on how to bring up your puppy. This will come from dog-owning friends, neighbors, and through articles and books you may read on the subject. Some of the advice will be sound, some will be nothing short of rubbish. What you should do above all else is to keep an open mind and let common sense prevail over prejudice and worn-out ideas that have been handed down over the centuries. There is no one way that is superior to all others, no more than there is no one dog that is exactly a replica of another. Each is an individual and must always be regarded as such.

A dog never becomes disobedient, unruly, or a menace to society without the full consent of his owner. Your puppy may have many limitations, but the singular biggest limitation he is confronted with in so many instances is his owner's inability to understand his needs and how to cope with them.

Opposite: The strong-minded Tibetan Spaniel is infamous for his escape attempts, so make sure your Tibbie is kept in a fenced-in yard and wears identification tags at all times.

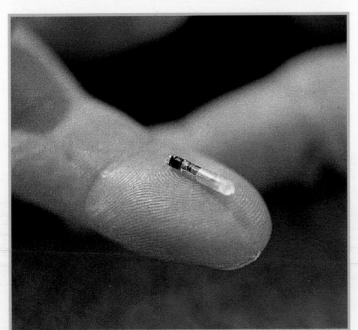

The newest method of identification is the microchip, a computer chip that is no bigger than a grain of rice, that is injected into the dog's skin.

IDENTIFICATION

It is a sad reflection on our society that the number of dogs and cats stolen every year runs into many thousands. To these can be added the number that get lost. If you do not want your cherished pet to be lost or stolen, then you should see that he is carrying a permanent identification number, as well as a temporary tag on his collar.

Permanent markings come in the form of tattoos placed either inside the pup's ear flap, or on the inner side of a pup's upper rear leg. The number given is then recorded with one of the national registration companies. Research laboratories will not purchase dogs carrying numbers as they realize these are clearly someone's pet, and not abandoned animals.

Have a clear and recent photograph of your dog to distribute in case he should become lost. Phari Ave Maria owned by Marti E. Smith.

As a result, thieves will normally abandon dogs so marked and this at least gives the dog a chance to be taken to the police or the dog pound, when the number can be traced and the dog reunited with its family. The only problem with this method at this time is that there are a number of registration bodies, so it is not always apparent which one the dog is registered with (as you provide the actual number). However, each registration body is aware of his competitors and will normally be happy to supply their addresses. Those holding the dog can check out which one you are with. It is not a perfect system, but until such is developed it's the best available.

A temporary tag takes the form of a metal or plastic disk large enough for you to place the dog's name and your phone number on it—maybe even your address as well. In virtually all places you will be required to obtain a license for your puppy. This may not become applicable until the pup is six months old, but it might apply regardless of his age. Much depends upon the state within a country, or the country itself, so check with your veterinarian if the breeder has not already advised you on this.

FEEDING YOUR TIBETAN SPANIEL

Tibbies are usually good eaters, neither finicky nor greedy. I recommend feeding your Tibbie a high quality dry food as his main source of nutrition. Because a Tibbie's teeth are usually crowded into a small muzzle, and sometimes crooked, crunching the dry food helps prevent tartar from building up. Balls of canned food make a good treat and are useful for giving medication.

I advise feeding your Tibbie puppy a food formulated for growing puppies until he is one year old.

Show your Tibetan Spaniel puppy you care by providing him with a high-quality dog food formulated especially for growth.

After that, switch to a food formulated for adults. When he reaches nine or ten years of age, you may want to consider switching to a food formulated for senior dogs.

Dog owners today are fortunate in that they live in an age when considerable cash has been invested in the study of canine nutritional requirements. This means dog food manufacturers are very concerned about ensuring that their foods are of the best quality. The result of all of their studies, apart from the food itself, is that dog owners are bombarded with advertisements telling them why they must purchase a given brand. The number of products available to you is unlimited, so it is hardly surprising to find that dogs in general suffer from obesity and an excess of vitamins, rather than the reverse. Be sure to feed age-appropriate food—puppy food up to one year of age, adult food thereafter. Generally breeders recommend dry food supplemented by canned, if needed.

FACTORS AFFECTING NUTRITIONAL NEEDS

Activity Level. A dog that lives in a country environment and is able to exercise for long periods of the day will need more food than the same breed of dog living in an apartment and given little exercise.

Quality of the Food. Obviously the quality of food will affect the quantity required by a puppy. If the

POPpups™ are 100% edible and enhanced with dog-friendly ingredients like liver, cheese, spinach, chicken, carrots, or potatoes. They contain no salt, sugar, alcohol, plastic or preservatives. You can even microwave a POPpup™ to turn into a huge crackly treat for your Tibetan Spaniel.

nutritional content of a food is low then the puppy will need more of it than if a better quality food was fed.

Balance of Nutrients and Vitamins. Feeding a puppy the correct balance of nutrients is not easy because the average person is not able to measure out ratios of one to another, so it is a case of trying

Carrots are rich in fiber, carbohydrates, and vitamin A. The Carrot Bone™ by Nylabone® is a durable chew containing no plastics or artificial ingredients and it can be served as-is, in a bone-hard form, or microwaved to a biscuit consistency. Your Tibetan Spaniel will love it.

to see that nothing is in excess. However, only tests, or your veterinarian, can be the source of reliable advice.

Genetic and Biological Variation. Apart from all of the other considerations, it should be remembered that each puppy is an individual. His genetic make-up will influence not only his physical characteristics but also his metabolic efficiency. This being so, two pups from the same litter can vary quite a bit in the amount of food they need to perform the same function under the same conditions. If you consider the potential combinations of all of these factors then you will see that pups of a given breed could vary quite a bit in the amount of food they will need. Before discussing feeding quantities it is valuable to know at least a little about the composition of food and its role in the body.

COMPOSITION AND ROLE OF FOOD

The main ingredients of food are protein, fats, and carbohydrates, each of which is needed in

relatively large quantities when compared to the other needs of vitamins and minerals. The other vital ingredient of food is, of course, water. Although all foods obviously contain some of the basic ingredients needed for an animal to survive, they do not all contain the ingredients in the needed ratios or type. For example, there are many forms of protein, just as there are many types of carbohydrates. Both of these compounds are found in meat and in vegetable matter—but not all of those that are needed will be in one particular meat or vegetable. Plants, especially, do not contain certain amino acids that are required for the synthesis of certain proteins needed by dogs.

Likewise, vitamins are found in meats and vegetable matter, but vegetables are a richer source of most. Meat contains very little carbohydrates. Some vitamins can be synthesized by the dog, so do not need to be supplied via the food. Dogs are carni-

A well-balanced diet will be evident in your Tibbie's shiny coat and overall healthy appearance. Fin. Ch. Bellezza's Cemeicca owned by Aino-Inkeri Huurinainen.

vores and this means their digestive tract has evolved to need a high quantity of meat as compared to humans. The digestive system of carnivores is unable to break down the tough cellulose walls of plant matter, but it is easily able to assimilate proteins from meat.

In order to gain its needed vegetable matter in a form that it can cope with, the carnivore eats all of its prey. This includes the partly digested food within the stomach. In commercially prepared foods, the cellulose is broken down by cooking. During this process the vitamin content is either greatly reduced or lost altogether. The manufacturer therefore adds vitamins once the heat process has been completed. This is why commercial foods are so useful as part of a feeding regimen, providing they are of good quality and from a company that has prepared the foods very carefully.

Proteins

Roar-Hide® is completely edible and is high in protein (over 86%) and low in fat (less than one-third of 1%). Unlike common rawhide, it is safer, less messy, and more fun for your Tibbie.

These are made from amino acids, of which at least ten are essential if a puppy is to maintain healthy growth. Proteins provide the building blocks for the puppy's body. The richest sources are meat, fish and poultry, together with their by-products. The latter will include milk, cheese, yogurt, fishmeal, and eggs. Vegetable matter that has a high protein content includes soy beans, together with numerous corn and other plant extracts that have been

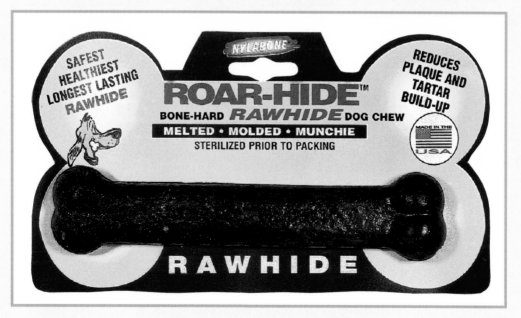

dehydrated. The actual protein content needed in the diet will be determined both by the activity level of the dog and his age. The total protein need will also be influenced by the digestibility factor of the food given.

Fats

These serve numerous roles in the puppy's body. They provide insulation against the cold, and help buffer the organs from knocks and general activity shocks. They provide the richest source of energy, and reserves of this, and they are vital in the transport of vitamins and other nutrients, via the blood, to all other organs. Finally, it is the fat content within a diet that gives it palatability. It is important that the fat content of a diet should not be excessive. This is because the high energy content of fats (more than twice that of protein or carbohydrate) will increase the overall energy content of the diet. The puppy will adjust its food intake to that of its energy needs, which are obviously more easily met in a high-energy diet. This will mean that while the fats are providing the energy needs of the puppy, the overall diet may not be providing its protein, vitamin, and mineral needs,

Because a Tibbie's teeth are usually crowded in a small muzzle, crunching on dry dog food will help prevent tartar from forming. Be sure to have clean water available at all times as well.

so signs of protein deficiency will become apparent. Rich sources of fats are meat, their byproducts (butter, milk), and vegetable oils, such as safflower, olive, corn or soy bean.

Carbohydrates

These are the principal energy compounds given to puppies and adult dogs. Their inclusion within most commercial brand dog foods is for cost, rather than dietary needs. These compounds are more commonly known as sugars, and they are seen in simple or complex compounds of carbon, hydrogen, and oxygen. One of the simple sugars is called

Put your dog on a regular feeding schedule as soon as possible. Depending on his lifestyle, an adult Tibetan Spaniel like Aust. Ch. Tygil Dikki can usually be fed twice a day. Owners, Judy and Tim Gard.

glucose, and it is vital to many metabolic processes. When large chains of glucose are created, they form compound sugars. One of these is called glycogen, and it is found in the cells of animals. Another, called starch, is the material that is found in the cells of plants.

Vitamins

These are not foods as such but chemical compounds that assist in all aspects of an animal's life. They help in so many ways that to attempt to describe these effectively would require a chapter in itself. Fruits are a rich source of vitamins, as is

The breeder will have started your puppy on the road to good nutrition. So if your decide to make any changes in your Tibbie's diet, do so gradually. Ch. Sierra Honey Bun At Nanjo owned by Nancy Cook.

the liver of most animals. Many vitamins are unstable and easily destroyed by light, heat, moisture, or rancidity. An excess of vitamins, especially A and D, has been proven to be very harmful. Provided a puppy is receiving a balanced diet, it is most unlikely there will be a deficiency, whereas hypervitaminosis (an excess of vitamins) has become quite common due to owners and breeders feeding unneeded supplements. The only time you should feed extra vitamins to your puppy is if your veterinarian advises you to.

Minerals

These provide strength to bone and cell tissue, as well as assist in many metabolic processes. Examples are calcium, phosphorous, copper, iron, magnesium, selenium, potassium, zinc, and sodium. The recommended amounts of all minerals in the diet has not been fully established. Calcium and phosphorous are known to be important, especially to puppies. They help in forming strong bone. As with vitamins, a mineral deficiency is most unlikely in pups given a good and varied diet. Again, an excess can create problems—this applying equally to calcium.

Water

This is the most important of all nutrients, as is easily shown by the fact that the adult dog is made up of about 60 percent water, the puppy containing an even higher percentage. Dogs must retain a water balance, which means that the total intake should be balanced by the total output. The intake comes either by direct input (the tap or its equivalent), plus water released when food is oxidized, known as metabolic water (remember that all foods contain the elements hydrogen and oxygen that recombine in the body to create water). A dog without adequate water will lose condition more rapidly than one depleted of food, a fact common to most animal species.

AMOUNT TO FEED

The best way to determine dietary requirements is by observing the puppy's general health and physical appearance. If he is well covered with flesh, shows good bone development and muscle, and is an active alert puppy, then his diet is fine. A puppy will consume about twice as much as an adult (of the same breed). You should ask the breeder of your puppy to show you the amounts fed to their pups and this will be a good starting point.

The puppy should eat his meal in about five to seven minutes. Any leftover food can be discarded or placed into the refrigerator until the next meal (but be sure it is thawed fully if your fridge is very cold).

If the puppy quickly devours its meal and is clearly still hungry, then you are not giving him enough food. If he eats readily but then begins to pick at it, or walks away leaving a quantity, then you are probably giving him too much food. Adjust this at the next meal and you will quickly begin to appreciate what the correct amount is. If, over a number of weeks, the pup starts to look fat, then he is obviously overeating; the reverse is true if he starts to look thin compared with others of the same breed.

The amount of food your Tibetan Spaniel requires will depend on his age, energy level and the activities in which he participates. Owners, M.C. Hourihane and D. Jenkins.

WHEN TO FEED

It really does not matter what times of the day the puppy is fed, as long as he receives the needed quantity of food. Puppies from 8 weeks to 12 or 16 weeks need 3 or 4 meals a day. Older puppies and adult dogs should be fed twice a day. What is most important is that the feeding times are reasonably regular. They can be tailored to fit in with your own timetable—for example, 7 a.m. and 6 p.m. The dog will then expect his meals at these times each day. Keeping regular feeding times and feeding set amounts will help you monitor your puppy's or dog's health. If a dog that's normally enthusiastic about mealtimes and eats readily suddenly shows a lack of interest in food, you'll know something's not right.

TRAINING YOUR TIBETAN SPANIEL

CRATE TRAINING

Tibbies are naturally clean and easy to housetrain provided *you* follow some simple guidelines. It is widely accepted that crate training is a foolproof method of housetraining. When you cannot supervise your puppy, place him in a wire crate. The correct size for a Tibbie puppy is about 24" x 20" x 20". The puppy learns that his crate is his "den," and dogs instinctively

Crate training is the quickest and easiest method of housebreaking your Tibetan Spaniel.

avoid soiling their "dens." The crate also keeps him out of other trouble, such as chewing up your belongings. How long the puppy can hold his urine and feces while in his crate depends on his age. A 10-week-old pup (the age at which most Tibbie puppies go to their new homes) may be able to "hold" only two or three hours, while a 16-week-old could wait for four or five hours. However, *never* leave a Tibbie puppy in his crate for more than four hours.

Besides using the crate for times when you can't watch him, it is also important to put your puppy on a schedule of feeding, potty and play times. Stick to the schedule, even on weekends. Take him outside when he first gets up and just before you put him to bed. Also, take him outside about a half hour after each meal and at regular intervals through the day. When you leave for work or otherwise cannot supervise the puppy, place him in his crate.

Always praise your puppy enthusiastically for "doing his business" in the proper place at the proper time. If your puppy has an "accident" in his crate or in the house, he may be ill. Otherwise, it's probably your fault. Either you failed to adhere to the schedule, the schedule is not realistic for your puppy, or you are not supervising or crating him properly. Unless you catch him the act, *never* scold your puppy for an accident.

It is important that your Tibbie spends time outdoors in order to enjoy the fresh air and sunshine.

Just clean it up when he isn't watching and resolve to do better next time.

I prefer training my Tibbies to "go" outdoors rather than on paper in the house. Although you can train your Tibbie either way, my advice is to choose one method or the other rather than to expect him to sometimes go on paper inside and to go outdoors at other times.

When your puppy demonstrates that you can trust him, begin leaving him unsupervised outside his crate for short periods. However, leave the open crate nearby as he will enjoy it as a "den" for the rest of his

The versatile Tibbie can excel at anything! Ch. Nittni's Whimsical Creation, CD, AX, AD, TT, TDI not only holds an obedience title and advanced agility titles, she is also a certified therapy dog. Owner, Karen Chamberlain.

life. Many people continue to confine the Tibbie to the kitchen or similar area during this transitional period. Gradually increase the length of time you leave him. If he begins to have accidents again, you're pushing him too fast. Back up and begin using the crate again.

EDUCATING TIBBIES

All Tibbies need some basic training. If you can trust your Tibbie to reliably obey your commands, he is a better companion for you and less likely to come to harm. A great goal for every Tibbie is to become a Canine Good Citizen. This is a program administered

by the American Kennel Club or corresponding national organizations in other countries. Passing the Canine Good Citizen test proves that a dog knows how to behave properly around strangers and other dogs and understands basic obedience commands. Many Tibbies are Canine Good Citizens and entitled to the title CGC after their names. In fact, passing the CGC test (or an equivalent) is usually a prerequisite to working as a therapy dog.

Aust. Ch. Toreana Junki has over 2000 Australian championship points to his credit and is a fine example of an educated Tibbie. Owners, Ken and Pam Talbot.

Tibbies are willing and able to learn quickly. The key to success is knowing how to work with your Tibbie's independent personality. Your job is to convince him that it's worth his while to do what you want and let him think it was his idea in the first place. Lessons must be fun and rewards plentiful.

Beginning in puppyhood, introduce your Tibbie to as many different sizes and shapes of dogs and people as possible. This process is called socialization. It is extremely important for a Tibbie's socialization to be a totally positive experience. The dogs he meets should be friendly and reliable and the people (including children) should be calm and welcoming. Your Tibbie should also learn to walk quietly on a lead, whether alone with you or in a crowd. He should allow people to pet, groom and examine him. He should tolerate trips in the car. He must also understand and obey certain basic commands such as "come," "sit" and "stay."

The voice commands you give must be consistent—the same word every time— and everyone in the family must use the same word(s). Speak firmly but quietly. Shouting, whining and pleading are ineffective. Also, avoid repeating commands because this teaches your Tibbie to ignore your voice. It has been my experience that Tibbies respond more reliably to commands in the form of hand signals than to the voice commands alone. A hand signal is simply a gesture. There are some standard signals, but it doesn't really matter how you signal as long as you are consistent. For example, the signal for "stay" is placing the palm of your hand in front of the Tibbie's face, and the signal for "come" is sharply bringing your palm toward yourself. A hand signal seems to grab a Tibbie's attention. Eventually, you may not need to give the voice command at all.

Teaching a Tibbie to do what you want *when you want it done* sometimes proves to be a challenge. Assuming he knows what you want, he may comply promptly, stare at you defiantly or flash a grin and run

Ch. Jemari Joyous Pippin, NA, TT, TDI demonstrates the "Heel" with her owner Karen Chamberlain.

the other way. It depends on how he feels at the moment. That's his independent streak showing. To counteract your Tibbie's independence, you must understand and apply positive training techniques.

Almost all Tibbies are highly food-motivated—in other words, they work for food. Use food in training! First, *show* your Tibbie, rather than tell him, what you want him to do. To help him understand, tempt him with a treat, such as a small piece of biscuit. When he does what you want, reward him with the treat. For example, to teach the "sit," let him sniff a small treat in your hand, then slowly move it up and back over his head. (Incidentally, the motion of your hand becomes the "sit" hand signal.) As his nose follows the treat, his

This Tibbie shows the dexterity and agility of the Tibetan Spaniel by clearing the bar jump. Owners, M.C. Hourihane and D. Jenkins.

rump will automatically fall into a sit. When he sits down, give him the treat as a reward and praise him profusely.

In the beginning, reward and praise your Tibbie even if he only partially does what you want. This builds his confidence and gives him a sense of success. Then, gradually begin to withhold the treat until he performs more promptly and correctly.

Enthusiastic praise is important, but praise-only training rarely (if ever) works with Tibbies as well as it

Well-mannered Tibetan Spaniels will be welcomed in any household. Batu Life Of The Parti and Ch. Batu Parti Until Dawn owned by Billie Ponton.

does with breeds that are less independent. When you first teach your Tibbie a behavior, always give the food reward first, then praise him a moment later. Eventually, you'll be able to omit the treat, but you should never take your Tibbie's obedience for granted. Always reward him with praise. Now and then, reinforce your praise by adding a treat as a surprise. If your Tibbie starts to ignore you, revert to rewarding him with treats.

The most effective training for Tibbies, hands down, is the click-and-treat method. It works, and Tibbies *love* it. When the Tibbie performs correctly, the trainer instantly snaps a handheld clicker and gives a food treat. Fascinated by the clicking game, the smart Tibbie soon connects the sound of the click with the food reward. Eventually, he learns to work for the click, with only the occasional food reward as a reminder. Click-and-treat training for Tibbies is fun, not a chore.

Tibbies like to lead. If a Tibbie thinks it was his idea in the first place, he will learn better and faster. It is inadvisable to use any form of force, such as jerking the Tibbie's lead or pushing his body into a position. With this breed, force is almost always ineffective and, worse, may produce exactly the opposite effect to what you desire. The highly insulted Tibbie may actually defy you. The more you force, the more he resists. At the very least, he will begin to mistrust you, and that is very sad indeed.

Tibbies do not require many repetitions to learn a new lesson. Once they understand what you want, they bore easily and will simply stop listening if you keep hammering away at it. Keep your lessons short and sweet. Change up the pace. Although you should continue to practice and reinforce each lesson you teach periodically throughout your Tibbie's life, always keep him guessing about what comes next. He'll love you for it.

Imagine that you are opening the door to leave for work one morning when your Tibbie slips by you and streaks toward the busy street. When you shout "come," will he turn and run back to you? Your "come" command must be irresistible: it's a matter of his life

Teaching your Tibetan Spaniel to walk on lead is important not only for his safety but for the safety of others. Int./Nord./Fin. Ch. Bio-Bio's Ivanhoe owned by Lisa Molin.

or death. Let's look at how to teach a Tibbie to "come" with positive techniques.

Have a yummy treat in one hand. Crouch down in front of your Tibbie, smile, hold out your arms, call "come" enthusiastically and give the hand signal with your treat hand. If he doesn't respond instantly, show him that treat. As soon as he moves toward you, begin praising to encourage him and, when he reaches you, give the treat and more praise. Have a friend on the other side of the room do the same. When the Tibbie is reliably going back and forth between the two of you, put him on a long lead and take him outside where there are more distractions. Repeat the whole routine. Reinforce this lesson frequently, in various places with differing distractions. Someday, your Tibbie will "test" you by lagging or ignoring you when you call "come." Get him back on track by adding a really exciting stimulus to the routine. Shaking a can with coins in it or blowing a whistle always brings mine running. Be creative. Educating your intelligent, independent Tibbie is a game of wits— it's up to you to win the game.

Who knows how far your Tibetan Spaniel can go? Shavarin's Doremi owned by Tiina Pentinmäki is a puppy with potential.

BREED CONCERNS

The Tibetan Spaniel is a long-lived, healthy breed. With good food, regular exercise, safety precautions and routine veterinary care, you can reasonably expect your Tibbie to lead an active life well into his mid-teens.

Most Tibbies die of the conditions that we associate with "old age" in dogs (and people)— namely, kidney or heart failure resulting from the wear and tear of a long life. Along the way, a Tibbie may suffer from a few health problems; a bout of flea allergy, the occasional gastrointestinal upset or an ear infection perhaps— like most any dog. However, those of special concern to breeders and owners of Tibetan Spaniels merit mention here.

DISEASES AND DISORDERS

Congenital disorders are present when a puppy is born. They may be inherited (or influenced by heredity

Sw. Ch. Mavibos Mardi, a top-winning veteran in Sweden, was 10 ¹/₂ years old when this photo was taken. Owner, Bodel Olsén.

in some way) or they may result from a problem that occurs before the puppy is born. However, some inherited problems do not show up until much later, when the dog is several months or even several years old.

The most common congenital defect in Tibbies is the umbilical hernia, a weakness in the abdominal wall at the site of the navel. Small ones are generally repaired when the puppy is spayed or neutered. Patellar luxation, sometimes called a "slipping knee-cap" (stifle), occurs fairly often in all small breeds. In Tibbies, the cases are usually mild and require no treatment. Distichiasis, extra eyelashes that may irritate the eye, is frequently found in Tibbies. For example, 11% of American Tibbies examined between 1991 and 1994 had distichiasis. Fortunately, most cases are mild, causing no symptoms or only a little tearing. In severe cases, the extra eyelashes may be surgically removed to relieve the irritation.

It appears that allergies are on the upswing among dogs as well as people and Tibbies are likewise affected. Flea allergy is the most common type, followed by inhalant allergy (hypersensitivity to airborne substances, such as pollen or dust) and food allergy (hypersensitivity to certain ingredients). The itchiness and chewing at the paws that Tibbie owners often report are sometimes due to boredom but may also be a sign of one or more allergies. Discuss these signs with your veterinarian. Treatment depends on the type of allergy involved.

Anecdotal evidence strongly suggests that intervertebral disk disease, a fairly common spinal disorder in small dogs, affects many Tibbies. Also called "slipped" or "herniated disk," it may result either from trauma (such as a fall) or from inherited factors. A disk is a structure that acts as a cushion between the vertebrae. When the outer shell of the disk tears, the gel-like substance inside leaks out and presses on the spinal cord. If your Tibbie experiences pain in the back or neck, get him to a veterinarian immediately. Treatment depends on the severity but usually entails cage rest and corticosteroid therapy.

The inherited disease that greatly concerns Tibetan Spaniel breeders worldwide is progressive retinal atrophy (PRA), a condition that causes gradual blindness in adults. PRA is neither painful nor life-threatening. Although fewer than 100 cases have been reported in Tibbies, all prospective parents should be tested before they are mated. Anyone considering a Tibbie puppy should discuss PRA with the breeder.

Another inherited condition that deserves attention is juvenile kidney disease, a general term for conditions in which the kidneys form cysts or fail to develop properly. Although rare in our breed, affected puppies and young adults eventually suffer kidney failure and die.

It is interesting to note that canine hip dysplasia, a scourge of many dog breeds, is not currently considered a significant problem in the Tibetan Spaniel. Only a minuscule number of cases of have been reported around the world.

Cherry eye is a red protrusion at the inner corner of the eye caused by the swelling of the underlying tear gland. The cause is unknown but may be related to stressful events such as teething.

Over one-quarter of unspayed females and those spayed after their second heat cycle develop mammary tumors. Of these, half are malignant. To minimize the risk, have your female Tibbie spayed before her first heat cycle and check her often for lumps. Early detection and treatment are critical.

Tradition among breeders holds that the Tibetan Spaniel may react adversely to anesthesia. This belief is shared by breeders of other short-muzzled breeds and other Tibetan breeds. Although no clinical

Gizmo owned by Alma Estrada and Tim Biancalana suffers from dry eye or sicca keratoconjuctivitis in one eye. Some cases of dry eye result from the surgical removal of a tear gland in treating cherry eye. This type of surgery is no longer recommended.

evidence exists to suggest that sensitivity to anesthetics is widespread in our breed, individual dogs may nonetheless react adversely. This reaction may be anaphylactic or it may result from an undetected, underlying problem, such as liver or kidney malfunction. Although improved anesthetics are now available, tests to screen for underlying problems before your Tibbie undergoes surgery may be advisable. Discuss your concerns with your veterinarian.

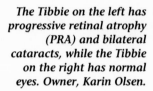

The Tibbie on the left has progressive retinal atrophy (PRA) and bilateral cataracts, while the Tibbie on the right has normal eyes. Owner, Karin Olsen.

CARING FOR SENIOR TIBBIES

Because Tibbies are long-lived, most owners must eventually care for a senior Tibbie. Although he retains his youthful outlook well into advanced years, the elderly Tibbie sooner or later slows down and sleeps more. As his discomforts multiply, he may become a little grumpy. His hearing and vision may deteriorate. He may forget his housetraining now and then. These are all normal signs of aging.

It is important to take your senior to the veterinarian for a checkup twice, rather than once, a year. Many ailments associated with old age are treatable. A biannual checkup enables the vet to identify and deal with any such problems quickly.

At home, watch your Tibbie's weight and make sure he continues to get moderate exercise. It may be advisable, for example, to change his diet to a higher fiber product formulated for older dogs. Make him comfortable with good bedding, such as egg-crate foam, placed in a warm spot. Because an older dog's skin and coat tend to be dry and itchy, groom your senior more often to keep the skin and coat in good condition. Be patient, and don't forget to lavish lots of love and affection on him.

75

YOUR HEALTHY TIBETAN SPANIEL

Dogs, like all other animals, are capable of contracting problems and diseases that, in most cases, are easily avoided by sound husbandry—meaning well-bred and well-cared-for animals are less prone to developing diseases and problems than are carelessly bred and neglected animals. Your knowledge of how to avoid problems is far more valuable than all of the books and advice on how to cure them. Respectively, the only person you should listen to about treatment is your vet. Veterinarians don't have all the answers, but at least they are trained to analyze and treat illnesses, and are aware of the full implications of treatments. This does not mean a few old remedies aren't good standbys when all else fails, but in most cases modern science provides the best treatments for disease.

Opposite: Veterinarians are trained to analyze and treat illnesses. Having complete trust in your chosen veterinarian is tantamount to the long life of your dog.

PHYSICAL EXAMS

Your puppy should receive regular physical examinations or check-ups. These come in two forms. One is obviously performed by your vet, and the other is a day-to-day procedure that should be done by you. Apart from the fact the exam will highlight any problem at an early stage, it is an excellent way of socializing the pup to being handled.

To do the physical exam yourself, start at the head and work your way around the body. You are looking for any sign of lesions, or any indication of parasites on the pup. The most common parasites are fleas and ticks.

It is important to maintain your Tibetan Spaniel's good health. Rivervalley's Tuka Zack-a-Ree owned by the Lorette family.

HEALTHY TEETH AND GUMS

Chewing is instinctual. Puppies chew so that their teeth and jaws grow strong and healthy as they develop. As the permanent teeth begin to emerge, it is painful and annoying to the puppy, and puppy owners must recognize that their new charges need something safe upon which to chew. Unfortunately, once the puppy's permanent teeth have emerged and settled solidly into the jaw, the chewing instinct does not fade. Adult dogs instinctively need to clean their teeth, massage their gums, and exercise their jaws through chewing.

It is necessary for your dog to have clean teeth. You should take your dog to the veterinarian at least once a year to have his teeth cleaned and to have his mouth examined for any sign of oral disease. Although dogs do not get cavities in the same way humans do, dogs'

The Hercules® by Nylabone® has raised dental tips that help fight plaque on your Tibetan Spaniel's teeth and gums.

teeth accumulate tartar, and more quickly than humans do! Veterinarians recommend brushing your dog's teeth daily. But who can find time to brush their dog's teeth daily? The accumulation of tartar and plaque on our dog's teeth when not removed can cause irritation and eventually erode the enamel and finally destroy the teeth. Advanced cases, while destroying the teeth, bring on gingivitis and periodontitis, two very serious conditions that can affect the dog's internal organs as well...to say nothing about bad breath!

Since everyone can't brush their dog's teeth daily or get to the veterinarian often enough for him to scale

Nylafloss® does wonders for your Tibetan Spaniel's dental health by massaging his gums and literally flossing between his teeth, loosening plaque and tartar build-up. Unlike cotton tug toys, Nylafloss® won't rot or fray.

the dog's teeth, providing the dog with something safe to chew on will help maintain oral hygeine. Chew devices from Nylabone® keep dogs' teeth clean, but they also provide an excellent resource for entertainment and relief of doggie tensions. Nylabone® products give your dog something to do for an hour or two every day and during that hour or two, your dog will be taking an active part in keeping his teeth and gums healthy…without even realizing it! That's invaluable to your dog, and valuable to you!

Nylabone® provides fun bones, challenging bones, and *safe* bones. It is an owner's responsibility to recognize safe chew toys from dangerous ones. Your dog will chew and devour anything you give him. Dogs must not be permitted to chew on items that they can break. Pieces of broken objects can do internal damage to a dog, besides ripping the dog's mouth. Cheap plastic or rubber toys can cause stoppage in the intestines; such stoppages are operable only if caught immediately.

The most obvious choices, in this case, may be the worst choice. Natural beef bones were not designed for chewing and cannot take too much pressure from the sides. Due to the abrasive nature of these bones, they should be offered most sparingly. Knuckle bones, though once very popular for dogs, can be easily

Nylabone® is the only plastic dog bone made of 100% virgin nylon, comes in many different sizes to suit all breeds of dog. The Souper Size, shown here, is for larger dogs. Your Tibetan Spaniel, of course, will need the petite or regular sizes.

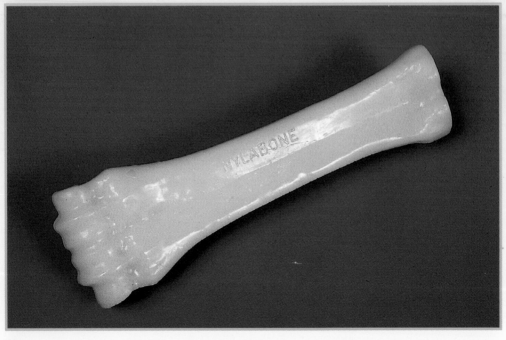

Chick-n-Cheez Chooz® are completely safe and nutritious health chews made from pure cheese protein, chicken, and fortified with vitamin E. They contain no salt, sugar, plastic, or preservatives and less than 1% fat.

chewed up and eaten by dogs. At the very least, digestion is interrupted; at worst, the dog can choke or suffer from intestinal blockage.

When a dog chews hard on a Nylabone®, little bristle-like projections appear on the surface of the bone. These help to clean the dog's teeth and add to the gum-massaging. Given the chemistry of the nylon, the bristle can pass through the dog's intestinal tract without effect. Since nylon is inert, no microorganism can grow on it, and it can be washed in soap and water or sterilized in boiling water or in an autoclave.

For the sake of your dog, his teeth and your own peace of mind, provide your dog with Nylabones®. They have 100 variations from which to choose.

FIGHTING FLEAS

Fleas are very mobile and may be red, black, or brown in color. The adults suck the blood of the host, while the larvae feed on the feces of the adults, which is rich in blood. Flea "dirt" may be seen on the pup as very tiny clusters of blackish specks that look like freshly ground pepper. The eggs of fleas may be laid on the puppy, though they are more commonly laid off the host in a favorable place, such as the bedding. They normally hatch in 4 to 21 days, depending on the temperature, but they can survive for up to 18 months if temperature conditions are not favorable. The larvae are maggot-like and molt a couple of times before forming pupae, which can survive long periods until the temperature, or the vibration of a nearby host, causes them to emerge and jump on a host.

There are a number of effective treatments available, and you should discuss them with your veterinarian, then follow all instructions for the one you choose. Any treatment will involve a product for your puppy or dog and one for the environment, and will require diligence on your part to treat all areas and thoroughly clean your home and yard until the infestation is eradicated.

THE TROUBLE WITH TICKS

Ticks are arthropods of the spider family, which means they have eight legs (though the larvae have six). They bury their headparts into the host and gorge on its blood. They are easily seen as small grain-like creatures sticking out from the skin. They are often picked up when dogs play in fields, but may also arrive in your yard via wild animals—even birds—or stray cats and dogs. Some ticks are species-specific, others are more adaptable and will host on many species.

The cat flea is the most common flea of dogs. It starts feeding soon after it makes contact with the dog.

The deer tick is the most common carrier of Lyme disease. Photo courtesy of Virbac Laboratories, Inc., Fort Worth, Texas.

The most troublesome type of tick is the deer tick, which spreads the deadly Lyme disease that can cripple a dog (or a person). Deer ticks are tiny and very hard to detect. Often, by the time they're big enough to notice, they've been feeding on the dog for a few days—long enough to do their damage. Lyme disease was named for the area of the United States in which it was first detected—Lyme, Connecticut—but has now been diagnosed in almost all parts of the U.S. Your veterinarian can advise you of the danger to your dog(s) in your area, and may suggest your dog be vaccinated for Lyme. Always go over your dog with a fine-toothed flea comb when you come in from walking through any area that may harbor deer ticks, and if your dog is acting unusually sluggish or sore, seek veterinary advice.

Attempts to pull a tick free will invariably leave the headpart in the pup, where it will die and cause an infected wound or abscess. The best way to remove ticks is to dab a strong saline solution, iodine, or alcohol on them. This will numb them, causing them to loosen their hold, at which time they can be removed with forceps. The wound can then be cleaned and covered with an antiseptic ointment. If ticks are common in your area, consult with your vet for a suitable pesticide to be used in kennels, on bedding, and on the puppy or dog.

INSECTS AND OTHER OUTDOOR DANGERS

There are many biting insects, such as mosquitoes, that can cause discomfort to a puppy. Many diseases are transmitted by the males of these species.

A pup can easily get a grass seed or thorn lodged between his pads or in the folds of his ears. These may go unnoticed until an abscess forms.

This is where your daily check of the puppy or dog will do a world of good. If your puppy has been playing in long grass or places where there may be thorns, pine needles, wild animals, or parasites, the check-up is a wise precaution.

SKIN DISORDERS

Apart from problems associated with lesions created by biting pests, a puppy may fall foul to a number of other skin disorders. Examples are ringworm, mange, and eczema. Ringworm is not caused by a worm, but is a fungal infection. It manifests itself as a sore-looking bald circle. If your puppy should have any form of bald patches, let your veterinarian check him over; a microscopic examination can confirm the condition. Many old remedies for ringworm exist, such as iodine, carbolic acid, formalin, and other tinctures, but modern drugs are superior.

Be sure to check your Tibbie's coat thoroughly for parasites such as fleas and ticks after he has been playing outside.

Fungal infections can be very difficult to treat, and even more difficult to eradicate, because of the spores. These can withstand most treatments, other than burning, which is the best thing to do with bedding once the condition has been confirmed.

Mange is a general term that can be applied to many skin conditions where the hair falls out and a flaky crust develops and falls away.

Often, dogs will scratch themselves, and this invariably is worse than the original condition, for it opens lesions that are then subject to viral, fungal, or parasitic attack. The cause of the problem can be various species of mites. These either live on skin debris and the hair follicles, which they destroy, or they bury themselves just beneath the skin and feed on the tissue. Applying general remedies from pet stores is not recommended because it is essential to identify the type of mange before a specific treatment is effective.

Eczema is another non-specific term applied to many skin disorders. The condition can be brought about in many ways. Sunburn, chemicals, allergies to foods, drugs, pollens, and even stress can all produce a deterioration of the skin and coat. Given the range of causal factors, treatment can be difficult because the problem is one of identification. It is a case of taking each possibility at a time and trying to correctly diagnose the matter. If the cause is of a dietary nature then you must remove one item at a time in order to find out if the dog is allergic to a given food. It could, of course, be the lack of a nutrient that is the problem, so if the condition persists, you should consult your veterinarian.

INTERNAL DISORDERS

It cannot be overstressed that it is very foolish to attempt to diagnose an internal disorder without the advice of a veterinarian. Take a relatively common problem such as diarrhea. It might be caused by nothing more serious than the puppy hogging a lot of food or eating something that it has never previously eaten. Conversely, it could be the first indication of a potentially fatal disease. It's up to your veterinarian to make the correct diagnosis.

The following symptoms, especially if they accompany each other or are progressively added to earlier symptoms, mean you should visit the veterinarian right away:

Continual vomiting. All dogs vomit from time to time and this is not necessarily a sign of illness. They will eat grass to induce vomiting. It is a natural cleansing process common to many carnivores. However, continued vomiting is a clear sign of a problem. It may be a blockage in the pup's intestinal tract, it may be induced by worms, or it could be due to any number of diseases.

Diarrhea. This, too, may be nothing more than a temporary condition due to many factors. Even a change of home can induce diarrhea, because this often stresses the pup, and invariably there is some change in the diet. If it persists more than 48 hours then something is amiss. If blood is seen in the feces, waste no time at all in taking the dog to the vet.

Running eyes and/or nose. A pup might have a chill and this will cause the eyes and nose to weep. Again, this should quickly clear up if the puppy is placed in a warm environment and away from any drafts. If it does not, and especially if a mucous discharge is seen, then the pup has an illness that must be diagnosed.

Coughing. Prolonged coughing is a sign of a problem, usually of a respiratory nature.

Wheezing. If the pup has difficulty breathing and makes a wheezing sound when breathing, then something is wrong.

Cries when attempting to defecate or urinate. This might only be a minor problem due to the hard state of the feces, but it could be more serious, especially if the pup cries when urinating.

Cries when touched. Obviously, if you do not handle a puppy with care he might yelp. However, if he cries even when lifted gently, then he has an internal problem that becomes apparent when pressure is applied to a given area of the body. Clearly, this must be diagnosed.

Refuses food. Generally, puppies and dogs are greedy creatures when it comes to feeding time. Some might be more fussy, but none should refuse more than one meal. If they go for a number of hours without showing any interest in their food, then something is not as it should be.

General listlessness. All puppies have their off days when they do not seem their usual cheeky, mischievous selves. If this condition persists for more than two days then there is little doubt of a problem. They may not show any of the signs listed, other than perhaps a reduced interest in their food. There are many diseases that can develop internally without displaying obvious clinical signs. Blood, fecal, and other tests are needed in order to identify the disorder before it reaches an advanced state that may not be treatable.

WORMS

There are many species of worms, and a number of these live in the tissues of dogs and most other animals. Many create no problem at all, so you are not even aware they exist. Others can be tolerated in small levels, but become a major problem if they number more than a few. The most common types seen in dogs are roundworms and tapeworms. While roundworms are the greater problem, tapeworms require an intermediate host so are more easily eradicated.

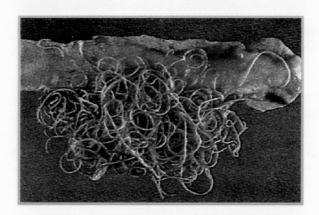

Roundworms are spaghetti-like worms that cause a pot-bellied appearance and dull coat, along with more severe symptoms, such as diarrhea and vomiting. Photo courtesy of Merck AgVet.

Roundworms of the species *Toxocara canis* infest the dog. They may grow to a length of 8 inches (20 cm) and look like strings of spaghetti. The worms feed on the digesting food in the pup's intestines. In chronic cases the puppy will become pot-bellied, have diarrhea, and will vomit. Eventually, he will stop eating, having passed through the stage when he always seems hungry. The worms lay eggs in the puppy and these pass out in his feces. They are then either ingested by the pup, or they are eaten by mice, rats, or beetles. These may then be eaten by the puppy and the life cycle is complete.

Larval worms can migrate to the womb of a pregnant bitch, or to her mammary glands, and this is how they pass to the puppy. The pregnant bitch can be wormed, which will help. The pups can, and should,

Whipworms are hard to find unless you strain your dog's feces, and this is best left to a veterinarian. Pictured here are adult whipworms.

be wormed when they are about two weeks old. Repeat worming every 10 to 14 days and the parasites should be removed. Worms can be extremely dangerous to young puppies, so you should be sure the pup is wormed as a matter of routine.

Tapeworms can be seen as tiny rice-like eggs sticking to the puppy's or dog's anus. They are less destructive, but still undesirable. The eggs are eaten by mice, fleas, rabbits, and other animals that serve as intermediate hosts. They develop into a larval stage and the host must be eaten by the dog in order to complete the chain. Your vet will supply a suitable remedy if tapeworms are seen or suspected. There are other worms, such as hookworms and whipworms, that are also blood suckers. They will make a pup anemic, and blood might be seen in the feces, which can be examined by the vet to confirm their presence. Cleanliness in all matters is the best preventative measure for all worms.

Heartworm infestation in dogs is passed by mosquitoes but can be prevented by a monthly (or daily) treatment that is given orally. Talk to your vet about the risk of heartworm in your area.

BLOAT (GASTRIC DILATATION)

This condition has proved fatal in many dogs, especially large and deep-chested breeds, such as the Weimaraner and the Great Dane. However, any dog can get bloat. It is caused by swallowing air during exercise, food/water gulping or another strenuous task. As many believe, it is not the result of flatulence. The stomach of an affected dog twists, disallowing food and blood flow and resulting in harmful toxins being released into the bloodstream. Death can easily follow if the condition goes undetected.

The best preventative measure is not to feed large meals or exercise your puppy or dog immediately after he has eaten. Veterinarians recommend feeding three smaller meals per day in an elevated feeding rack, adding water to dry food to prevent gulping, and not offering water during mealtimes.

VACCINATIONS

Every puppy, purebred or mixed breed, should be vaccinated against the major canine diseases. These are distemper, leptospirosis, hepatitis, and canine parvovirus. Your puppy may have received a temporary vaccination against distemper before you purchased him, but be sure to ask the breeder to be sure.

The age at which vaccinations are given can vary, but will usually be when the pup is 8 to 12 weeks old. By this time any protection given to the pup by antibodies received from his mother via her initial milk feeds will be losing their strength.

Rely on your veterinarian for the most effectual vaccination schedule for your Tibetan Spaniel puppy.

The puppy's immune system works on the basis that the white blood cells engulf and render harmless

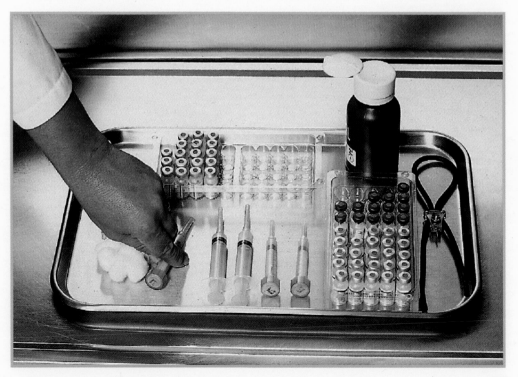

attacking bacteria. However, they must first recognize a potential enemy.

Vaccines are either dead bacteria or they are live, but in very small doses. Either type prompts the pup's defense system to attack them. When a large attack then comes (if it does), the immune system recognizes it and massive numbers of lymphocytes (white blood corpuscles) are mobilized to counter the attack. However, the ability of the cells to recognize these dangerous viruses can diminish over a period of time. It is therefore useful to provide annual reminders about the nature of the enemy. This is done by means of booster injections that keep the immune system on its alert. Immunization is not 100-percent guaranteed to be successful, but is very close. Certainly it is better than giving the puppy no protection.

Dogs are subject to other viral attacks, and if these are of a high-risk factor in your area, then your vet will suggest you have the puppy vaccinated against these as well.

Your puppy or dog should also be vaccinated against the deadly rabies virus. In fact, in many places it is illegal for your dog not to be vaccinated. This is to protect your dog, your family, and the rest of the animal population from this deadly virus that infects the nervous system and causes dementia and death.

ACCIDENTS

All puppies will get their share of bumps and bruises due to the rather energetic way they play. These will usually heal themselves over a few days. Small cuts should be bathed with a suitable disinfectant and then smeared with an antiseptic ointment. If a cut looks more serious, then stem the flow of blood with a towel or makeshift tourniquet and rush the pup to the veterinarian. Never apply so much pressure to the wound that it might restrict the flow of blood to the limb.

In the case of burns you should apply cold water or an ice pack to the surface. If the burn was due to a chemical, then this must be washed away with copious amounts of water. Apply petroleum jelly, or any vegetable oil, to the burn. Trim away the hair if need be. Wrap the dog in a blanket and rush him to the vet. The pup may go into shock, depending on the severity of the burn, and this will result in a lowered blood pressure, which is dangerous and the reason the pup must receive immediate veterinary attention.

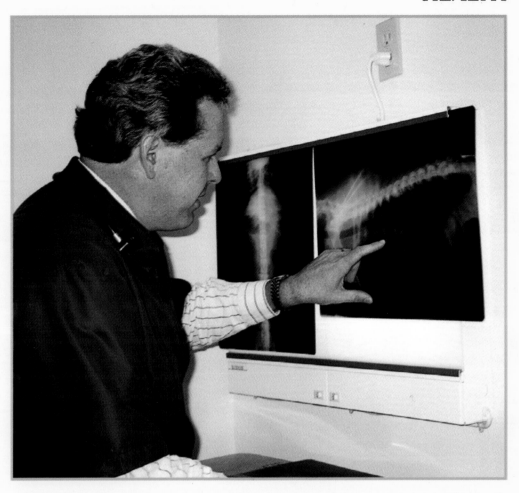

It is a good idea to x-ray the chest and abdomen on any dog hit by a car.

If a broken limb is suspected then try to keep the animal as still as possible. Wrap your pup or dog in a blanket to restrict movement and get him to the veterinarian as soon as possible. Do not move the dog's head so it is tilting backward, as this might result in blood entering the lungs.

Do not let your pup jump up and down from heights, as this can cause considerable shock to the joints. Like all youngsters, puppies do not know when enough is enough, so you must do all their thinking for them.

Provided you apply strict hygiene to all aspects of raising your puppy, and you make daily checks on his physical state, you have done as much as you can to safeguard him during his most vulnerable period. Routine visits to your veterinarian are also recommended, especially while the puppy is under one year of age. The vet may notice something that did not seem important to you.

91

PET OWNERS & BLOOD PRESSURE

Over the past few years, several scientific studies have documented many health benefits of having pets in our lives. At the State University of New York at Buffalo, for example, Dr. Karen Allen and her colleagues have focused on how physical reactions to psychological stress are influenced by the presence of pets. One such study compared the effect of pets with that of a person's close friend and reported pets to be dramatically better than friends at providing unconditional support. Blood pressure was monitored throughout the study, and, on average, the blood pressure of people under stress who were *with* their pets was 112/75, as compared to 140/95 when they were with the self-selected friends. Heart rate differences were also significantly lower when participants were with their pets. A follow-up study included married couples and looked at the stress-reducing effect of pets versus *spouses*, and found, once again, that pets were dramatically more successful than other people in reducing cardiovascular reactions to stress. An interesting discovery made in this study was that when the spouse and pet were *both* present, heart rate and blood pressure came down dramatically.

Other work by the same researchers has looked at the role of pets in moderating age-related increases in blood pressure. In a study that followed 100 women (half in their 20s and half in their 70s) over six months, it was found that elderly women with few social contacts and *no* pets had blood pressures that were significantly higher (averages of 145/95 compared to 120/80) than elderly women with their beloved pets but few *human* contacts. In other words, elderly women with pets, but no friends, had blood pressures that closely reflected the blood pressures of young women.

This series of studies demonstrates that pets can play an important role in how we handle everyday stress, and shows that biological aging cannot be fully understood without a consideration of the social factors in our lives.

More than best friends or even spouses, pets have a natural calming effect on their humans. This is Ch. Tibroke's Bon Appetite owned by Becky Maag.

SKULL — Slightly domed.

EARS
Well feathered.

STOP
Slight but defined.

EYES
Oval in shape.

MUZZLE
Blunt and free
from wrinkle.

**MANE OR
SHAWL**

WITHERS

SHOULDER

FORELEGS
Bones slightly bowed.

FEET
Hare-footed, small and neat.

*Ch. Ebonstern Avalon Dandi Lion owned by
Dr. Lee Nelson.*